# malays

## favourites

by Wendy Hutton

Delicious recipes from the crossroads of Asia—including popular Malaysian classics such as Black Pepper Crabs, Penang Spicy Rojak and Rendang Ayam.

PERIPLUS

# Basic Malaysian Ingredients

**Amaranth** is a leafy vegetable also known as Chinese spinach. It may be substituted with normal spinach. The leaves are usually green although some varieties are red. Whatever the colour, all types of amaranth taste the same.

**Bangkuang** is the Malay name for jicama. It is a large root, shaped like a top. It has a thin beige skin covering crisp, white flesh. It tastes slightly sweet and juicy when young but becomes fibrous as it gets older.

**Belachan**, the Malay name for dried shrimp paste, is a dense mixture of fermented ground prawns that must be toasted before use—either wrapped in foil and dry-roasted or toasted over a gas flame on the back of a spoon.

**Cardamom** is a highly aromatic pod containing tiny black seeds. If whole pods are used, they should be removed before serving. If seeds are called for, lightly smash the pods and take out the seeds. Ground cardamom is sold in packets or small tins.

Dried red chilies

Fresh finger-length chilies

Bird's-eye chilies

**Chillies** come in many sizes. Fresh green and red **finger-length chillies** are moderately hot. Tiny red, green or orange **chilli padi** (bird's eye chillies) are very hot. **Dried chillies** are usually deseeded, cut into lengths and soaked in warm water to soften before use. **Chilli powder** is made from ground dried chillies.

Coconut cream and **coconut milk** (*santan*) are used in many Asian desserts and curries. To obtain fresh coconut cream (which is normally used for desserts), grate the flesh of 1 coconut into a bowl (about 4 cups of grated coconut flesh), add $1/2$ cup water and knead thoroughly a few times, then strain with a muslin cloth or cheese cloth. **Thick coconut milk** is obtained by the same method but by adding double the water to the grated flesh (about 1 cup instead of $1/2$ cup). **Thin coconut milk** (which is used for curries rather than desserts) is obtained by pressing the coconut a second time, adding 1 cup of water to the same grated coconut flesh and squeezing it again. Although freshly pressed milk has more flavour, coconut cream and milk are now widely sold canned or in packets that are tasty and convenient.

**Curry leaves** are sold in sprigs with 8–15 small, green leaves and are so-called because they are used to flavour Indian curries.

**Curry powder** is made from various combinations of ground spices that generally include cumin, coriander seeds, turmeric and chilli. Different spice combinations are used for meat, poultry and fish. Curry powders used for meats and poultry contain stronger tasting spices such as cloves, cinnamon and black pepper. Fish curry powder usually omits these. Curry powders are sold in packets in supermarkets or mixed on the spot in wet market stalls.

**Dried prawns** are best kept refrigerated in a humid climate. Look for brightly-coloured, plump prawns. Soak for about 5 minutes to soften.

**Dried black Chinese mushrooms** must be soaked in hot water to soften before use, from about 15 minutes to 1 hour, depending on the thickness of the caps.

**Galangal** is an aromatic root used throughout most of Southeast Asia, known as *lengkuas* in Singapore and Malaysia, as *laos* in Indonesia and as *kha* in Thailand. The fresh root can be sliced and deep-frozen for future use.

**Ghee** is a rich clarified butter oil with the milk solids removed that is the main oil used in Indian cooking. Substitute with vegetable oil or butter.

**Hay koh** is also known as black prawn paste and is sometimes labelled *petis*. This thick black paste has a strong fishy taste and is used in some *nonya* dishes such as Penang Laksa and Rojak sauce.

**Kaffir lime leaves** (daun limau purut) are added whole to curries, or finely shredded and added to salads, giving them a citrusy flavour. Available frozen or dried in supermarkets.

Dark Soy Sauce     Light Soy Sauce

**Soy sauce** is probably the best known Asian seasoning, brewed from soybeans, wheat and salt. It is available in several forms—light, dark and sweet. Light or "regular" soy sauce is used in most recipes in this book. It is saltier, less malty in flavour and thinner than black soy sauce. Soy sauce is available in bottles—in supermarkets and provision shops.

**Kangkung** is a highly nutritious leafy green vegetable also known as water spinach. Young shoots may be eaten raw as part of a salad platter or with a dip. The leaves and tender stems are often braised with chilli and spices.

**Lap cheong**, or sweet, dried Chinese sausages are perfumed with rose-flavoured wine. They are never eaten alone, but sliced and cooked with rice or other foods.

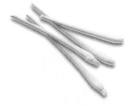

**Lemongrass** or citronella is a lemon-scented stem which grows in clumps. Each plant resembles a miniature leek. Use only the thicker bottom one third of the lemongrass stem, remove and discard the dry outer leaves, and use only the tender inner part of the stem. Lemongrass is available fresh in most supermarkets.

**Palm sugar** is made from the distilled juice of various palm fruits. Palm sugar varies in colour from golden to dark brown. It has a rich

flavour similar to dark brown sugar or maple syrup, which makes a good substitute.

**Pandanus leaves**, also known as pandan leaves, are long, thin leaves used to impart a delicate fragrance and green hue to cakes and desserts. Substitute bottled pandanus essence or vanilla essence.

**Plum sauce** is a reddish-brown jam made from plums, vinegar and sugar. It is sold in bottles and small tins, and is normally eaten with strong meats such as roast duck.

**Rice wine** is often used in Chinese cooking, as a tenderizer, to blend flavours and to enhance taste. The

4

best wine for Chinese cooking is *hua diao* rice wine, Japanese *sake* or *mirin*. A good alternative is dry sherry.

**Sesame oil** is extracted from sesame seeds that have been well toasted, producing a dark, dense, highly aromatic oil that can be used for marinades, sauces and soups, or as a table condiment.

Its nutty, smokey flavour has become a hallmark of Chinese cuisine.

**Star anise** is an eight-pointed dried tree pod encasing shiny black seeds with a strong aniseed (licorice) flavour. The whole spice is used and discarded just before serving.

**Tamarind pulp** is the pulpy flesh surrounding

hard, black seeds in the large, brown pods of the tamarind tree. It has a sour fruity taste, and is often used as a flavouring. It can be bought fresh or dried still in the pod, or in compressed blocks, with the seeds already removed. **Tamarind juice** adds a fruity sourness to sauces and soups. Soak 1 tablespoon tamarind pulp in 60 ml ($^1/_4$ cup) water, then squeeze and strain the mixture to obtain the juice.

Soft tofu

Firm tofu

Pressed tofu
(*Tau kwa*)

Deep fried tofu
(*Tau pok*)

**Tofu** or bean curd comes in various form. **Soft tofu** is silky and smooth whereas **firm tofu** is denser and stronger in flavour. *Tau kwa* is firm tofu that has been compressed to expel most of the moisture. **Tofu skin** is the dried skin that forms on top of boiling soy milk; it is dried and sold in sheets as a wrapper, or as *tau fu kee*, a thick twisted skin added to meat or vegetable dishes. Small squares of **fermented tofu** are sold in jars. They are either red on the outside, if flavoured with chilli and spices, or creamy white and used as a condiment with rice porridge. Another type of bean curd sometimes added to braised dishes or soups is dried-fried bean curd, *tau pok,* which is generally sold in small rectangles. These are often sold on strings in Asia, but are elsewhere usually packed in plastic. They are light and spongy in texture, and need to be dipped briefly in boiling water to remove the oil before being used. Dried deep-fried bean curd has an almost nutty flavour and is particularly appreciated for the way it soaks up the liquid to which it is added. It can be kept refrigerated for at least two weeks.

# Seasonings used in Bah Kut Teh (Pork Ribs Soup)

These seasonings are commonly sold in packets in supermarkets in Singapore and Malaysia, pre-measured for one batch of Bah Kut Teh, as per the recipe on page 21. They may be purchased individually in Chinese apothecary shops.

**Codonopsis dangshen** is a mild-tasting and sweet herb that is said to nourish the blood. It is sometimes used as a substitute for ginseng.

**Solomon's seal** or *yu ju* is a perennial herb with edible leaves and roots. The medicinal root comes in brittle, twisted pieces that are yellow or light brown. It is said to stimulate the appetite.

**Ligusticum wallichii** or *chuan xiong* is an herb whose leaves are used to expel intestinal parasites. The bitter roots of this herb are most often used in Chinese medicine to purify the blood and promote circulation.

**Black dried dates** or *hei zao* are the fruits of a spiny shrub. Dates are often used in Chinese medicine to nourish the blood.

**Rehmannia glutinosa** or *gan di huang* is a perennial herb. Its dried root is sold in large chunks and is said to promote muscle growth.

**Chinese wolfberries** or *gou ji zi* are sweet reddish fruits that are sold dried. They resemble tiny red currants and are said to nourish the liver and kidneys and improve vision.

# Chicken Stock

1 teaspoon oil
1 clove garlic, smashed
  and chopped
$1/2$ chicken or 2 chicken
  carcasses chopped in
  half, skin and fats
  discarded
$2^1/_2$ litres (10 cups)
  water
1 medium onion,
  chopped
2 spring onions,
  chopped
4 thin slices ginger
10 black peppercorns
$1/_2$ teaspoon salt

1 Put the oil in a large pan and heat. Add the garlic and stir-fry over low heat until golden brown. Lift out the garlic and discard, leaving the garlic-flavoured oil in the pan. Add the chicken and water. Bring to the boil then simmer uncovered for 10 minutes, skimming off any scum that rises to the surface.

2 Add all other ingredients, cover the pan and simmer very gently for 1 hour. Remove the lid and continue simmering until the stock is reduced by half, about another hour. Do not let the stock boil, or the result will be cloudy rather than clear.

3 Strain the stock into a large bowl, cool, then refrigerate for several hours. Scrape off any fat that solidifies on the surface, then transfer the stock into a covered container. If not using immediately, refrigerate or deep-freeze.

*A faster alternative to making true chicken stock is to use chicken stock cubes prepared according to the package instructions, although this will not taste the same.*

# Crispy-fried Shallots

$1/_2$ cup (125 ml) oil
6–8 shallots, peeled and
  thinly sliced

1 Heat oil in a saucepan over medium heat and fry the sliced shallots until golden brown, taking great care not to over-brown them as this makes them taste bitter.

2 Remove the fried shallots with a slotted spoon, transferring them onto a plate lined with paper towels. If not using them immediately, store in a dry, airtight jar to preserve their crispness.

# Lobah (Deep-fried Pork and Prawn Rolls)

400 g (14 oz) lean pork shoulder, cubed
250 g ($^1/_2$ lb) fresh prawns, peeled and deveined
60 ml ($^1/_4$ cup) water
1 small carrot, grated (about 85 g/$^1/_4$ cup)
4 shallots, chopped
2 stalks spring onions, chopped
6 water chestnuts, chopped
$^1/_2$ teaspoon salt
1 tablespoon ground white pepper
1 egg
1 heaped tablespoon cornflour
3 large sheets dried bean curd skin
Oil for deep-frying
Bottled plum sauce or chilli sauce

**1** Put the pork and prawns in a food processor and pulse until coarsely ground. Bring water to the boil in a small saucepan, then add carrots and boil for 2 minutes. Drain and add the carrots, shallots, spring onions, water chestnuts, salt, pepper, egg and cornflour to the pork mixture. Pulse until the mixture becomes a paste, then transfer to a bowl.
**2** Wipe each bean curd sheet with a clean damp cloth, then cut into 15-cm (6-in) squares. Put a little of the mixture into the centre of each piece of bean curd skin, shaping into a horizontal roll. Tuck in the ends, then roll up and press gently to seal.
**3** Heat the oil in a wok. Deep-fry the rolls, a few at a time, until golden brown and crisp, 4–5 minutes. Drain on paper towel and serve with bottled plum sauce or chilli sauce.

Serves 4
Preparation time: **30 mins**
Cooking time: **15–20 mins**

# Penang Spicy Rojak

1 small cucumber, skin
raked with a fork, cut
in irregular bite-sized
pieces
1 small *bangkuang* (yam
bean) (about 250 g/
9 oz), peeled and cut in
bite-sized pieces
1 square *tau pok* (deep-
fried bean curd squares),
cut in bite-sized pieces
2 small unripe (green)
mangoes, peeled and
cut in bite-sized pieces
4 *jambu air* (water
apples), quartered
(optional—see note)
1 thick slice fresh pineapple (about 200 g/7oz),
cut in bite-sized pieces
1 small torch ginger bud
(*bunga siantan*), thinly
sliced (optional, see
note)
75 g unsalted dry-roasted
peanuts, crushed (about
$^1/_2$ cup)
2 tablespoons sesame
seeds, toasted until
golden brown

**Sauce**
8 dried red chillies, sliced
and soaked in hot water
to soften
4 tablespoons *hae koh*
(black prawn paste)
1 teaspoon *belachan*
(dried prawn paste),
toasted (see page 3)
1 tablespoon hot water
1 tablespoon dark soy
sauce
60 ml ($^1/_4$ cup) tamarind
juice (see page 5)
1 tablespoon sugar
$^1/_2$ teaspoon salt
(optional)

Serves 6–8
Preparation time: **45 mins**
Cooking time: **10 mins**

1 To make the Sauce, grind the chillies to a smooth
paste in a blender, food processor or mortar and pestle.
Add all other ingredients except salt and blend well.
Taste and add salt if desired.
2 Put the cucumber, *bangkuang, tau pok*, mangoes,
*jambu air* and pineapple in a bowl. Pour over the
Sauce and toss, then transfer to a serving dish and
scatter with the torch ginger bud (if using), peanuts
and sesame seeds. Serve immediately.

*Jambu air* or water apples are small rose-coloured fruits
with thin edible skins and crisp, white flesh. The jambu
air is juicy and may be eaten raw. It has a slightly
sweet taste. Tart green apples are a good substitute.
**Torch ginger buds**, also known as bunga siantan or
bunga kantan, are the edible pink buds of a wild ginger plant. It is eaten raw with a dip, added to salads
or used in soups and curries. It has no substitute. If
you are not using fresh buds immediately, they may
be frozen whole.

# Prawn Fritters (Cucur Udang)

3 tablespoons rice flour
2 tablespoons plain
  flour
2 eggs, lightly beaten
1 tablespoon water
$1/2$ teaspoon salt
1 clove garlic, smashed
  and finely chopped
1 teaspoon very finely
  chopped ginger
1 spring onion, finely
  chopped
1 large red chilli, seeded
  and finely chopped
  (optional)
$1/4$ teaspoon ground
  white pepper
600 g ($1 1/4$ lbs) fresh
  medium prawns,
  peeled and deveined,
  finely chopped
Oil for deep-frying

1 Put both types of flour in a mixing bowl and stir in the eggs, water, salt, garlic, ginger, spring onions, chilli and pepper, mixing until smooth. Add the prawns and stir to mix well.

2 Heat the oil in a wok and when hot, drop in table-spoons of batter and cook until golden brown, about 1–2 minutes. Drain on paper towel and serve hot.

*Rice flour* is made by grinding uncooked rice grains. This cream-coloured flour is sold in packets and is available in supermarkets. It can also be made in small quantities by placing rice grains in a blender or food processor.

Serves 4
Preparation time: **15 mins**
Cooking time: **15 mins**

# Salt and Pepper Crabs

2–3 fresh crabs
  (about 1 kg/2 lbs)
125 g (1 cup) flour
1 tablespoon salt
1 tablespoon freshly
  ground black pepper
1 tablespoon powdered
  sugar
Oil for deep-frying

Serves 4
Preparation time: **15 mins**
Cooking time: **15 mins**

1 Put the crabs in the freezer for about 30 minutes if still alive to immobilise them. Pull off the underneath flap (pointed for male crabs, rounded for females) then carefully remove the back. Chop each crab in half lengthwise with a cleaver and remove the spongy grey matter inside the shell. Remove the claws and crack in several places with a cleaver. Cut each half into 2–3 pieces, leaving the legs attached. Rinse the crab and drain thoroughly.

2 Combine the flour, salt, pepper and sugar in a large plastic bag. Add half the crab pieces, hold the neck of the bag tightly and shake gently to coat the crab pieces. Transfer to a colander and flour the remaining crab.

3 Heat the oil in a wok until very hot. Add half the crab pieces and deep-fry until bright red and cooked, about 6–7 minutes. Cook the remaining crab pieces, drain on a paper towel and serve hot.

# Baby Kailan with Salted Fish

400 g (14 oz) baby *kailan*, halved lengthwise
3 tablespoons oil
20 g salted fish, chopped, soaked in hot water and drained (3 tablespoons)
2¹/₂ cm (1 in) ginger, thinly sliced
¹/₂ teaspoon salt
1 teaspoon soy sauce
1 tablespoon rice wine
3 tablespoons chicken stock (page 7), one small stock cube dissolved in 3 tablespoons hot water, or 1 tablespoon oyster sauce

Serves 4
Preparation time: **20 mins**
Cooking time: **15 mins**

**1** Wash and rinse the baby *kailan*, discarding the outer leaves if they are too hardy. Trim off the bottom 1 cm (¹/₄ in) of the baby *kailan* stalk.
**2** Heat the oil in a frying pan over high heat. Reduce heat to medium, stir-fry the fish until crispy, about 6–10 minutes, then set aside.
**3** Stir-fry the ginger for about one minute, then add the *kailan*, salt, soy sauce, wine and chicken stock or oyster sauce. Stir-fry for 5–7 minutes over high heat.
**4** Add the salted fish, stir quickly, then dish vegetables onto a plate and serve hot with rice.

*Baby kailan* are young and tender kailan buds that are usually cooked whole.
*Salted fish* should be soaked in hot water for 15 minutes before cooking to reduce its saltiness.

# Kangkung Tumis Belachan

450 g (1 lb) *kangkung*
(water convolvulus)
³/₄ teaspoon *belachan*
(dried prawn paste),
toasted until dry and
crumbly (see page 3)
125 ml (¹/₂ cup) warm
water
1 teaspoon rice wine
1 tablespoon oil
1 medium red or brown
onion, sliced
2 cloves garlic, smashed
and finely chopped
1 red chilli, sliced

Serves 4
Preparation time: **15 mins**
Cooking time: **5 mins**

**1** Wash the *kangkung* in several changes of water to remove grit. Cut the stalks and leaves into 5-cm (2-in) lengths. Discard the tough lower portion of the stalks. Drain and set aside.

**2** Put the *belachan* into a small bowl and mash using the back of a spoon. Add the water and rice wine and stir until the *belachan* is dissolved.

**3** Heat the oil in a wok for 30 seconds. When it is moderately hot, add the onion, garlic and chilli and stir-fry for 2 minutes. Put in the *kangkung* and stir-fry for 1 minute, mixing thoroughly.

**4** Add the *belachan* mixture to the wok. Cook, stirring frequently, until the *kangkung* is tender, about 3 minutes. Serve hot.

*If* kangkung *is not available, it may be substituted with spinach, a leafy green vegetable sold fresh in wet markets and supermarkets.*

# Cucumber and Pineapple Kerabu

1 small cucumber
1 teaspoon salt
2 large slices fresh pineapple (about 250 g/9 oz), cored and diced
2 tablespoons torch ginger (*bunga siantan*), sliced (optional, see note)

**Dressing**
4 tablespoons dried prawns, soaked to soften
1–2 red chillies, sliced
1 teaspoon *belachan* (dried prawn paste), toasted (see page 3)
1–2 tablespoons lime juice
2 tablespoons water
1 tablespoon sugar
1 teaspoon salt

1 Rake the skin of the cucumber with a fork and rub all over with the salt. Rinse under running water, squeeze the cucumber, then cut into 1-cm ($^1/_2$-in) cubes. Put in a bowl with the pineapple and torch ginger, if desired.
2 To make the Dressing, put all the ingredients in a spice grinder or blender and process until finely ground. Add to the cucumber and pineapple, toss and serve immediately.

*Torch ginger buds*, also known as bunga siantan or bunga kantan, are the edible pink buds of a wild ginger plant. It is eaten raw with a dip, added to salads or used in soups and curries. It has no substitute. If you are not using fresh buds immediately, they may be frozen whole.

Serves 4
Preparation time: **20 mins**

# Long Beans Stir-fried with Dried Prawn Sambal

2 tablespoons dried prawns, soaked in hot water to soften
4 shallots, chopped
2 large red chillies, sliced
2 cloves garlic
1 teaspoon *belachan* (dried prawn paste), toasted (see page 3)
2 tablespoons oil
400 g (14 oz) long beans or green beans, cut in bite-sized lengths
60 ml ($^1/_4$ cup) water
$^1/_2$ teaspoon salt, or more to taste

**1** Grind the dried prawns, shallots, chillies, garlic and *belachan* in a spice grinder or blender or mortar and pestle, until mashed but not turned into a smooth paste.
**2** Heat the oil in a wok and add the ground *belachan* mixture. Stir-fry over low–medium heat until fragrant, about 4 minutes. Increase the heat, add the long beans and stir-fry until well coated, about 1 minute.
**3** Add 60 ml ($^1/_4$ cup) of the water and salt and stir-fry the beans over high heat, adding more water as required. Cook until the beans are tender and all the water has evaporated, then serve hot with plain rice.

Serves 4–6
Preparation time: 20 mins
Cooking time: 8 mins

# Sweet Potato and Spinach in Coconut Milk

6 shallots, chopped
2 large red chillies, sliced
$^1/_2$ teaspoon *belachan* (dried prawn paste)
2 tablespoons oil
1 tablespoon dried prawns, soaked in hot water to soften
500 ml (2 cups) coconut milk
$^1/_2$ teaspoon salt, or more to taste
400 g (14 oz) sweet potato, peeled and cut in bite-sized chunks
150 g (5 oz) spinach or amaranth leaves, coarse stems discarded

1 Grind the shallots, chillies and *belachan* in a spice grinder, blender or mortar and pestle until fine, adding a little oil if needed to keep the mixture turning.
2 Heat the oil in a large saucepan and stir-fry the ground ingredients over low-medium heat, 4 minutes. Add the dried prawns and stir-fry 2 minutes. Pour in the coconut milk and bring to the boil over medium heat, stirring frequently.
3 Add salt and sweet potato and simmer uncovered for 10 minutes. Add spinach and continue simmering until the vegetables are cooked, about 5 minutes. Transfer to a serving dish and serve hot with rice.

*Pumpkin may be used instead of sweet potato, and 150 g (5 oz) long beans used instead of spinach.*

Serves 4
Preparation time: **25 mins**
Cooking time: **30 mins**

# Bah Kut Teh (Pork Ribs Soup)

3 litres (12 cups) water
10 cloves unpeeled garlic, washed
30 g (1 oz) packet *bah kut teh* seasonings (see page 6)
700 g (1$^1/_2$ lbs) pork ribs
6 dried black Chinese mushrooms, soaked in hot water
   for 10 minutes, stems discarded
100 g (3$^1/_2$ oz) button mushrooms (optional)
200 g Chinese cabbage, cut into 2-cm ($^3/_4$-in) sections
   and scalded with boiling water (about 2$^1/_2$ cups)
4 *tau pok* (fried bean curd squares) each sliced in half
4 tablespoons ($^1/_4$ cup) soy sauce
1 teaspoon sugar
1 sprig coriander leaves (cilantro) to garnish

**1** Put the water and garlic in a pot and bring to the
boil. Add herbs, chicken or pork ribs and both lots of
mushrooms. Return to the boil, then lower heat and
simmer over medium–low heat for 45 minutes or
until meat is tender.
**2** Add the cabbage, *tau pok*, soy sauce and sugar to
the pot.
**3** Dish into a casserole and garnish with coriander
leaves. Serve hot with hot rice and sliced red chillies
and dark soy sauce on the side.

Serves 4
Preparation time: **15 mins**
Cooking time: **45 mins–1 hour**

# Steamboat

250 g ($^1/_2$ lb) lean pork, thinly sliced

250 g ($^1/_2$ lb) beef, thinly sliced

250 g ($^1/_2$ lb) chicken meat, cut in bite-sized pieces

250 g ($^1/_2$ lb) white fish fillet, skinned and cubed

400 g (14 oz) fresh prawns, peeled and deveined, tails left on

100 g ($3^1/_2$ oz) firm *tofu*, cubed

8 dried black Chinese mushrooms, soaked in hot water for 10 minutes, stems discarded

200 g (7 oz) spinach or amaranth leaves

200 g (7 oz) long-leaf lettuce or Chinese cabbage

300 g (10 oz) dried rice vermicelli, soaked in hot water 10 minutes and boiled 1–2 minutes

4 eggs (optional)

## Seasoned Stock

$1^1/_2$ litres (6 cups) chicken stock (see page 7)

2 teaspoons rice wine

2 teaspoons sesame oil

$^1/_4$ teaspoon white pepper

1 tablespoon crispy-fried shallots (see page 7)

## Accompaniments

Soy sauce

Very finely grated fresh ginger

Bottled chilli sauce

Bottled plum sauce

Hot mustard

Crispy-fried shallots to serve (see page 7)

Serves 6–8
Preparation time: **50 mins**
Cooking time: **10 mins**

1 Prepare the Seasoned Stock by combining chicken stock, water, wine, oil and pepper in a large saucepan. Bring to the boil, lower heat and simmer 3 minutes. Just before cooking, transfer hot stock to a steamboat and add the crispy-fried shallots.

2 Arrange slices of pork, beef and chicken meat on a plate. Arrange fish, prawns, *tofu* and mushrooms on a separate plate. Wash and dry the spinach or amaranth and lettuce or Chinese cabbage and put on a plate.

3 Divide the vermicelli between 4 soup bowls. Prepare accompaniments by mixing soy sauce and ginger and dividing between 4 small sauce bowls. Divide chilli sauce, plum sauce and mustard between individual sauce bowls.

4 Place the stock-filled steamboat in the centre of the table. Each person dips portions of food to cook in the hot stock with either a small mesh basket or chopsticks, eating it with the various Accompaniments.

5 When the meat, fish, vegetables and *tofu* have been finished, ladle some of the reduced stock from the pot over each bowl of noodles. Break in a whole egg if desired, and serve to complete the meal.

*If using a charcoal steamboat, place it on top of a wooden board so the heat from the charcoal does not damage the table.*

# Char Kway Teow

100 g ($3^1/_2$ oz) hard pork fat (cut from the back), cut in
  tiny cubes, or 3 tablespoons oil (see note)
2 tablespoons water
4 cloves garlic, smashed and chopped
2 large red chillies, crushed to a paste
150 g ($5^1/_2$ oz) lean pork, sliced
150 g ($5^1/_2$ oz) fresh prawns, peeled and deveined
150 g ($5^1/_2$ oz) squid, thinly sliced
1 tablespoon light soy sauce
1 tablespoon dark soy sauce
2 teaspoons oyster sauce
$1/_2$ teaspoon salt
1 teaspoon ground white pepper
250 g (about 2 cups) bean sprouts
1 kg (2 lbs) fresh *kway teow* noodles or 300 g (10 oz)
  dried *hor fun* or river noodles, scalded in boiling
  water, rinsed and drained
1 large red chilli, sliced
Sprigs of fresh coriander leaves (cilantro), to garnish

**1** Put the pork fat and water in a wok and cook over
medium heat, stirring from time to time, until the
pieces of fat have turned crisp. Remove and drain on
paper towel. Leave 3 tablespoons of the pork oil in the
wok and discard the remainder.
**2** Heat the oil and stir-fry the garlic and chilli over
low–medium heat for about 30 seconds. Increase heat,
add the pork and stir-fry 2 minutes. Add the prawns
and squid and stir-fry another 2 minutes. Season with
both lots of soy sauce, oyster sauce, salt and pepper.
**3** Add the bean sprouts and stir-fry 2 minutes, then put
in the noodles and stir-fry until well mixed and heated
through. Stir in the crisp pork fat and transfer to a
serving dish. Garnish with chilli and coriander.

*For a healthier alternative, use 3 tablespoons oil instead
of the pork fat to fry the ingredients.*

Serves 6
Preparation time: **15 mins**
Cooking time: **10–15 mins**

# Spiced Lamb with Rice Biryani

2 tablespoons oil
1 cinnamon stick
(about 5 cm/2 in)
6 cloves
6 cardamom pods, slit
and bruised
$1/_2$ teaspoon freshly
ground black pepper
1 medium red or brown
onion, chopped
$1 1/_2$ teaspoons chopped
ginger
4 cloves garlic, chopped
3 tablespoons meat curry
powder
3 tablespoons water
750 g ($1 3/_4$ lbs) boneless
lean lamb, cubed
3 large tomatoes, chopped
125 ml ($1/_2$ cup) plain
yoghurt
125 ml ($1/_2$ cup) water
1 teaspoon salt
2 tablespoons finely
chopped mint
(optional)
4 cups uncooked basmati
rice, soaked and drained
1 tablespoon salt
1 tablespoon ghee

**Garnish**
2 tablespoons ghee or
butter
70 g ($1/_2$ cup) raw
cashews, split in half
70 g ($1/_2$ cup) raisins
3 tablespoons crispy-fried
shallots (see page 7)
Sprigs of fresh coriander
leaves (cilantro) or mint

**Milk Mixture**
2 tablespoons ghee
125 ml ($1/_2$ cup) cream or
evaporated milk
Pinch saffron strands
(optional)
Few drops rose essence

Serves 6
Preparation time: **30 mins**
Cooking time: **1 hour**

1 Heat the oil in a saucepan and add the cinnamon, cloves, cardamom and pepper. Stir-fry over low–medium heat for 2 minutes, then add the onions, ginger and garlic. Stir-fry until the onions start to soften, about 4 minutes. Mix curry powder and water, then add to the pan and stir-fry 2 minutes. Put in the lamb and stir-fry until it changes colour and the liquid dries up, about 5 minutes.
2 Add tomatoes and cook until they start to soften, 2–3 minutes. Add yoghurt and mix. Pour water, then add salt and mint. Bring to the boil, cover and simmer until lamb is tender and 60 ml ($1/_4$ cup) sauce is left in the pan.
3 Put the water and salt into a large pot and bring to the boil. When boiling, stir in the rice with a wooden spoon. Bring the water back to the boil, then simmer uncovered for 5 minutes. Drain the rice in a large sieve.
4 To prepare the Garnish, heat the ghee in a small pan and stir-fry the cashews until golden. Drain and set aside. Add raisins to the ghee left in the pan and cook for 1 minute. Mix with the cashews and crispy-fried shallots, then divide into 2 portions.
5 To assemble biryani, melt 1 tablespoon ghee in a large oven-proof casserole with a lid, swirling so that the sides are greased. Put the partly-cooked rice in a large bowl and stir in half the Garnish ingredients, mixing well. Spread half the rice in the casserole and arrange the lamb evenly over the top. Spoon over the remaining rice. The biryani can be set aside for several hours.
6 To prepare the Milk Mixture, melt the butter and combine with evaporated milk, food colouring and rose essence. Spoon this evenly over the top of the prepared biryani. Cover the casserole then transfer to an oven preheated to 150°C (302°F) and cook for 30 minutes. Transfer to a large plate and sprinkle the remaining Garnish ingredients and coriander.

# Quick Tomato Rice

2 tablespoons ghee or
  butter
1 medium onion,
  chopped
2 cloves garlic, smashed
  and finely chopped
1 star anise
2 cloves
1 cinnamon stick
  (about 5 cm/2 in)
2 cups uncooked long
  grain rice, washed and
  drained
1 cup (250 ml) canned
  concentrated tomato
  soup
1 1/2 cups (375 ml) water
1/2 teaspoon salt
3 tablespoons crispy-fried
  shallots (see page 7)
1 stalk spring onions,
  finely chopped

1 Heat the ghee or butter in a medium saucepan and
stir-fry the onion, garlic, star anise, cloves and cinnamon until the onion softens and turns transparent,
3 minutes. Add the rice and stir well to coat the grains
with the ghee. Add the tomato soup, water and salt
and bring to the boil. Stir the rice, reduce the heat
slightly and partially cover the saucepan. Simmer
until all the liquid has been absorbed and small bub-
bles appear on the surface of the rice, about 6 minutes.
2 Reduce the heat to low, cover the saucepan and let
the rice cook for 10 minutes. Remove the saucepan
from the heat, uncover and wipe the moisture off the
inside of the lid. Fluff up the rice with a fork and
replace the lid. Let stand for 10–20 minutes.
3 Just before serving, transfer the rice to a serving
bowl and garnish with the shallots and spring onions.

Serves 4
Preparation time: **15 mins**
Cooking time: **40 mins**

# Claypot Rice with Chestnuts and Chicken

300 g (10 oz) chicken thighs, cut into bite-sized pieces
2 tablespoons oil
2 cups uncooked rice, washed and drained
1 heaped tablespoon finely shredded ginger
12 fresh or dried chestnuts, boiled until just soft, cut in half
2 dried *lap cheong* (Chinese sausages), cut diagonally in $^1/_2$-cm ($^1/_4$-in) slices
2 tablespoons crispy-fried shallots (see page 7)
2 tablespoons finely chopped spring onions

**Marinade**

1 tablespoon dark soy sauce
1 tablespoon oyster sauce
1 tablespoon rice wine
1 teaspoon sugar
1 teaspoon sesame oil
$^1/_2$ teaspoon cornflour

**1** Put chicken pieces in a bowl and stir in all Marinade ingredients. Set aside to marinate for 20 minutes.
**2** Heat the oil in a large claypot. Add the rice and stir over medium heat until the rice is well coated, about 1 minute. Add sufficient water to cover the rice by 2 cm ($^3/_4$ in). Bring to the boil over high heat, then cook with the pot uncovered until the water has been absorbed and "craters" appear in the surface of the rice, about 5 minutes. Add the ginger, chestnuts and marinated chicken pieces, pushing them well into the rice. Lay the sliced *lap cheong* on top, cover and cook over low heat for 20 minutes; do not remove lid before this time.
**3** Stir the rice with a fork or chopstick, cover and cook over very low heat until the chicken is done and the rice is dry, about 15 minutes. Garnish with the crispy-fried shallots and spring onions before serving. If desired, serve with a soup and vegetable dish with sliced red chillies and soy sauce on the side.

Serves 4
Preparation time: **35 mins + 20 mins for marinating**
Cooking time: **40 mins**

# Chilli-fried Prawns

450 g (1 lb) large prawns, shells intact
4 cm (1$^1/_2$ in) fresh ginger, chopped
1 teaspoon water
2 tablespoons light soy sauce
2 teaspoons dark soy sauce
3 teaspoons rice wine
2 teaspoons sugar
$^1/_2$ teaspoon sesame oil
2 stalks spring onions, roots discarded, tied in a knot
2 tablespoons oil
60 ml ($^1/_4$ cup) water
1 large red chilli, chopped
Few sprigs fresh coriander leaves (cilantro)

**1** Trim the feelers off the prawns, but leave on the heads and shells.
**2** Process the ginger and water in a spice grinder or mortar and pestle until finely ground. Transfer to a sieve held over a bowl and press down with the back of a spoon to extract as much ginger juice as possible. Stir in both lots of soy sauce, rice wine, sugar and sesame oil. Add the spring onions and prawns, stirring to mix well. Leave to marinate at least 30 minutes.
**3** Drain prawns, reserving the marinade. Heat the oil in a wok until smoking hot. Add the prawns and stir-fry for 2 minutes. Add the water, reserved marinade and salt and cook, stirring frequently, until the prawns are done, 2–3 minutes. Transfer to a serving dish and garnish with chopped chilli and coriander leaves.

Serves 4–6
Preparation time: **15 mins + 30 mins for marinating**
Cooking time: **5 mins**

# Crystal Prawns

450 g (1 lb) prawns,
  peeled and deveined
1 teaspoon baking soda
4 teaspoons cornflour
$^1/_2$ teaspoon salt
1 teaspoon sugar
1 egg white, whisked
2 tablespoons oil
1 teaspoon ginger,
  chopped

**Sauce**
125 ml ($^1/_2$ cup) chicken
  stock (see page 7)
1 tablespoon rice wine
1 tablespoon oyster sauce
1 teaspoon cornflour

Serves 4
Preparation time: **15 mins**
Cooking time: **5 mins**

**1** Put the prawns in a bowl. Sprinkle with baking
soda and cornflour. Massage firmly by hand for
2 minutes to ensure a firm texture after cooking.
Sprinkle salt and sugar over the prawns, then stir in
egg white. Marinate 5 minutes. Drain and set aside.
Combine all Sauce ingredients in a bowl and set aside.
**2** Heat oil in a wok. Add ginger and stir-fry for 10
seconds. Add the prawns and stir-fry over high heat
until just cooked, 2–3 minutes.
**3** Stir the Sauce mixture then add to the wok. Lower
heat slightly and stir until the sauce thickens and
clears, about 30 seconds. Serve immediately.

*If desired, add fresh asparagus. Cut the tender part of
a small bunch of asparagus spears into 3-cm lengths.
Stir-fry over high heat in 1 tablespoon oil for 15 seconds. Add 3 tablespoons water, cover the wok and
cook 2 minutes. Remove from the wok and set aside.
Prepare prawns as directed, adding asparagus to the
wok just before adding the prepared sauce mixture.*

# Black Pepper Crabs

3 fresh crabs (about 1 kg/2 lbs)
5 tablespoons oil
2 tablespoons butter
4 shallots, thinly sliced
4 cloves garlic, chopped
1 tablespoon *tau cheo* (salted soybean paste), mashed
1 tablespoon dried prawns, roasted and ground
2 tablespoons coarsely ground black pepper
10 curry leaves
5–10 red or green bird's-eye chillies, chopped
125 ml ($^1/_2$ cup) water
2 tablespoons dark soy sauce
2 tablespoons sugar
1 tablespoon oyster sauce
Few sprigs coriander leaves (cilantro), to garnish

**1** Clean the crabs and cut in half, discarding the spongy grey matter inside the shell. Smash the claws with a cleaver to allow the seasonings to penetrate.
**2** Heat the oil in a large pan. Add crabs and stir-fry for 15 minutes on high heat, or until crabs are half-cooked. Remove, drain and set aside.
**3** Heat the pan again, add butter, shallots, garlic, *tau cheo*, dried prawns, pepper, curry leaves and chillies. Sauté until fragrant. Add a little water if the pan begins to dry up.
**4** Return crabs to the pan, then add soy sauce, sugar, and oyster sauce. Stir-fry for another 10 minutes on medium high heat. Add a little water if the sauce starts to dry up.
**5** Garnish with coriander leaves and serve at room temperature with hot rice.

> **Tau cheo** or salted soybean paste is a richly-flavoured seasoning that is sold in jars. The beans vary from dark brown to light golden in colour, and are sometimes labelled "yellow bean sauce". The beans are usually mashed with the back of a spoon before use.

Serves 4
Preparation time: **20 mins**
Cooking time: **30 mins**

# Ikan Moolie
## (Fish in Coconut Gravy)

8 shallots, chopped
3 large red chillies, chopped
1$^1/_2$ tablespoons oil
250 ml (1 cup) thin coconut milk
$^1/_2$ teaspoon turmeric powder
1 stem lemongrass, thick bottom half only, bruised and
  sliced in 3–4 pieces
2 thin slices *asam gelugor* (dried garcinia)
$^1/_2$ teaspoon salt
600 g (1$^1/_4$ lbs) white fish fillets
125 ml ($^1/_2$ cup) coconut cream

**1** Grind shallots and chillies to a paste in a spice grinder or mortar and pestle. Heat oil in a saucepan and add the paste. Stir-fry over low–medium heat, 4 minutes.
**2** Slowly stir in the thin coconut milk and turmeric, then add lemongrass, *asam gelugor* and salt. Bring to the boil, stirring constantly, then add the salt and simmer gently until the fish is cooked through, 5–8 minutes depending on the thickness of the fish.
**3** Add the coconut cream and heat. Stir gently until the sauce thickens, then transfer to a serving bowl. Serve with white rice.

**Asam gelugor** *or dried garcinia is used to provide a sourness to some Malay and Nonya dishes. It may be substituted with tamarind pulp.*

Serves 4
Preparation time: **15 mins**
Cooking time: **15 mins**

# Gulai Ikan (Sour and Spicy Fish Stew)

1 large or 2 small white pomfret, or 600 g (1¹/₄ lbs) fish steaks such as *ikan tenggiri* (Spanish mackerel)

3 tablespoons oil

60 ml (¹/₄ cup) tamarind juice (see page 5)

4 sprigs *daun kesum* (polygonum leaf, see note)

1 torch ginger bud (*bunga siantan*), halved lengthwise (optional, see note)

500–750 ml (2–3 cups) water

2 teaspoons sugar

1 teaspoon salt

**Seasoning Paste**

10–12 dried red chillies, sliced and soaked in hot water to soften

16 shallots, chopped

3 cm (1¹/₄ in) fresh galangal, chopped

2 stems lemongrass, thick inner part of bottom half only, sliced

2 cm (³/₄ in) fresh turmeric root, or ¹/₂ teaspoon turmeric powder

¹/₂ teaspoon *belachan* (dried prawn paste), toasted (see page 3)

1 Pat the fish dry with a paper towel. If using pomfret, cut in half diagonally. Set aside.

2 To prepare the Seasoning Paste, process all ingredients to a smooth paste in a spice grinder, adding a little oil if needed to keep the mixture turning.

3 Heat the oil in a saucepan. Add the Seasoning Paste and cook for 4–5 minutes, stirring often. Add the tamarind juice, *daun kesum*, torch ginger bud, water, sugar and salt. Bring to the boil, lower heat and simmer uncovered for 5 minutes.

4 Add the fish to the pan and enough water to cover the fish. Simmer until the fish is done. The fish should be white right through when tested with the tip of a knife. Taste and add more sugar or salt if desired. Serve with white rice.

*Daun kesum* or *polygonum* is a long-leafed herb with a strong, minty flavour. It is usually sold in bunches with pointed leaves on each stem.

*Torch ginger buds*, also known as bunga siantan or bunga kantan, are the edible pink buds of a wild ginger plant. It is eaten raw with a dip, added to salads or used in soups and curries. It has no substitute. If you are not using fresh buds immediately, they may be frozen whole.

Serves 4
Preparation time: 20 mins
Cooking time: 20 mins

# Spicy Stingray Grilled In Banana Leaf

1–2 wings (about 500 g/ 1 lb) stingray or whole snapper (see note)
3 tablespoons oil
60 ml (¹/₄ cup) tamarind juice (see page 5)
1 tablespoon soy sauce
1 teaspoon sugar
1–2 large pieces banana leaf, softened over a gas flame or in boiling water
4 small green limes, cut into wedges

## Seasoning Paste
6 dried red chillies, sliced and soaked in hot water to soften
2 large red chillies, chopped
10 shallots, chopped
2 cloves garlic
2 teaspoons *belachan* (dried prawn paste), toasted
1 teaspoon salt

1 Wash and dry the stingray wings. Make a slit along both sides of the central bony cartilage, from the central part almost to the wing tip, following the cartilage and taking care not to cut the wing completely in two. This makes it easier to remove the cooked flesh and helps the flavours penetrate the flesh.

2 Prepare the Seasoning Paste by grinding all ingredients to a smooth paste in a spice grinder or mortar and pestle. Heat oil in a wok then stir-fry the Seasoning Paste over low–medium heat until fragrant, about 4 minutes. Add tamarind juice, soy sauce and sugar and cook for 1 minute, stirring.

3 Allow Seasoning Paste to cool, then spread over both sides of the stingray, pushing some of the mixture into the slits. Wrap the stingray in a banana leaf and secure the leaf with toothpicks so that it does not open during grilling. Grill over hot charcoal or under a grill until cooked and the banana leaf is slightly charred; about 10 minutes. Serve with lime wedges for squeezing over the stingray before eating.

*If using a whole snapper, make diagonal slits on both sides of the fish. Spread the Seasoning Paste onto both sides of the fish, pushing some paste into each slit.*

Serves 4
Preparation time: **25 mins**
Cooking time: **20 mins**

# Squid with Spicy Prawn Filling

4 medium squids,
  (about 400 g/14 oz)

**Prawn Filling**
1–2 dried red chillies,
  sliced and soaked in hot
  water to soften
2 shallots, chopped
1 tablespoon oil
200 g (7 oz) small fresh
  prawns, peeled and
  deveined

**Sauce**
6 dried red chillies, sliced
  and soaked in hot water
8 shallots, chopped
2 slices galangal, chopped
1 clove garlic, chopped
2 tablespoons oil
60 ml ($^1/_4$ cup) tamarind
  juice (see page 5)
1 stem lemongrass, bot-
  tom half only, bruised
  and cut in 4 pieces
125 ml ($^1/_2$ cup) thick
  coconut milk
$^1/_2$ teaspoon salt

1 Peel the reddish skin off the squid and remove the heads. Cut off the tentacles just above the eyes, and squeeze to push out the bony portion in the centre of the tentacles. Reserve. Clean the body of the squid and drain. Set aside.

2 Prepare the Prawn Filling by grinding the chillies and shallots to a paste. Heat the oil in a small pan and stir-fry the paste for 4 minutes. Add the prawns and stir-fry until they change colour all over, about 2 minutes. Transfer the mixture to a bowl, cool slightly, then stuff some of it into the body of each cleaned squid.

3 To prepare the Sauce, grind the chillies, shallots, galangal and garlic to a smooth paste in a food processor or mortar and pestle, adding a little of the oil if needed to keep the mixture turning. Heat oil in wide pan and stir-fry the paste over low–medium heat until fragrant, about 4 minutes. Add the tamarind juice, lemongrass, thick coconut milk and salt and bring slowly to the boil, stirring. Add the stuffed squid and tentacles and simmer gently, uncovered, until the squid are cooked, about 5 minutes. Serve hot with rice.

Serves 4
Preparation time: **35 mins**
Cooking time: **15 mins**

# Chicken Steamed with Black Mushrooms

1 chicken, (about 1¹/₂ kg/
  3 lbs) cut in serving portions, or 1 kg (2 lbs)
  chicken pieces (breast,
  thigh and drumstick)
8 dried black Chinese
  mushrooms, soaked in
  hot water 10 minutes to
  soften, stems discarded
5 cm (2 in) fresh ginger,
  chopped
1 tablespoon water
2 tablespoons rice wine
1 tablespoon soy sauce
1 tablespoon oyster
  sauce
1 teaspoon sesame oil
1 teaspoon sugar
1 teaspoon salt
1 teaspoon ground white
  pepper
2 tablespoons finely
  sliced spring onions

**1** Put the chicken and mushrooms in a heat-proof bowl with a lid.

**2** Process the ginger and water in a spice grinder, or pound ginger in a mortar and mix with water to form a paste. Put the paste in a small sieve and press with the back of a spoon to extract the ginger juice. Sprinkle the ginger juice, rice wine, soy and oyster sauce, sesame oil, sugar, salt and pepper over the chicken and mushrooms, massaging with your hand to mix well. Stir, then cover and refrigerate 1 hour.

**3** Put the bowl inside a steamer filled with water, or place on a rack set in a deep saucepan half-filled with water. Steam over medium heat for 30–40 minutes, until the chicken is cooked, adding a little more boiling water to the steamer every 10 minutes. Transfer to a serving dish, garnish with spring onions and serve hot with plain rice.

Serves 4–6
Preparation time: **15 mins + 1 hour marinating time**
Cooking time: **30–40 mins**

# Kari Ayam (Mild Chicken Curry)

3 tablespoons chicken or
  meat curry powder
3 tablespoons water
6 shallots, chopped
3–4 cloves garlic,
  chopped
3 cm (1$^1/_4$ in) fresh
  ginger, chopped
60 ml ($^1/_4$ cup) oil
1 whole chicken (about
  1$^1/_2$ kg/3 lbs) cut in
  serving portions, or 1 kg
  (2 lbs) chicken pieces
$^1/_2$ cup freshly grated
  coconut (about 50 g),
  toasted in a dry pan
  until brown, processed
  until the oil comes out
1 whole star anise
2 cloves
1 cinnamon stick
  (about 3 cm/1$^1/_4$ in)
750 ml (3 cups) thin
  coconut milk
1 teaspoon salt
2 medium potatoes,
  peeled and quartered
2 medium ripe tomatoes,
  quartered

**1** Mix the curry powder with water to make a paste and set aside. Process the shallots, garlic and ginger to a smooth paste in a spice grinder, adding a little of the oil if necessary to keep the mixture turning.
**2** Heat the oil in a wok and stir-fry the processed mixture over low–medium heat, 4 minutes. Add the curry paste, stir-fry 2 minutes, then add chicken, grated coconut, star anise, cloves and cinnamon. Stir-fry for 2 minutes then add the thin coconut milk, salt and potatoes. Bring to the boil, stirring occasionally.
**3** Lower heat and simmer uncovered, stirring occasionally, until the chicken and potatoes are cooked, about 25 minutes, adding a little water if the sauce begins to dry. Add the tomatoes, simmer 4–5 minutes, then transfer to a serving dish.

Serves 4–6
Preparation time: 20 mins
Cooking time: 40 mins

# Rendang Ayam
## (Spicy Chicken in Coconut Gravy)

1 whole chicken (about $1\frac{1}{2}$ kg/3 lbs), cut in pieces
$1\frac{1}{2}$ litres (6 cups) thin coconut milk
250 ml (1 cup) coconut cream
1 teaspoon salt
1 teaspoon sugar
4 fresh kaffir lime leaves (*daun limau purut*), finely
   shredded (see note)
4 fresh turmeric leaves, finely shredded (optional)
3 pandan leaves, raked with a fork, tied into a knot

**Seasoning Paste**
10–15 dried red chillies, sliced, and soaked in hot water
16 shallots, chopped
6 cm ($2\frac{1}{2}$ in) ginger, chopped
6 cm ($2\frac{1}{2}$ in) galangal, chopped
6 cloves garlic, chopped

**1** To make the Seasoning Paste, grind all ingredients
in a spice grinder, blender or mortar and pestle until
fine, adding a little coconut milk if needed to keep the
mixture turning.
**2** Put the Seasoning Paste, chicken, coconut milk,
coconut cream, salt, sugar, kaffir leaves, turmeric and
pandan leaves into a wok and bring slowly to the boil,
stirring the liquid constantly to prevent curdling.
**3** Simmer uncovered, stirring occasionally, until the
chicken is tender and the coconut milk has thickened.
Discard pandan leaves and serve hot with white rice.

*If **fresh kaffir lime leaves** (daun limau purut) are not
available, use frozen kaffir lime leaves or substitute $\frac{1}{4}$
teaspoon grated lemon or lime skin for each lime leaf.*

Serves 4–6
Preparation time: **20 hours**
Cooking time: **1 hour**

# Chicken in Spicy Tomato Sauce

1 whole chicken (about
1 1/2 kg/3 lbs) or 1 kg
(2 lbs) chicken pieces,
cut in serving portions
1 teaspoon salt
1 teaspoon turmeric
powder
Oil for deep-frying
1 whole star anise
2 cloves
1 cinnamon stick
(about 2 cm/3/4 in)
250 ml (1 cup) thick
coconut milk
60 ml (1/4 cup) coconut
cream
3 tablespoons concen-
trated tomato paste
1 teaspoon sugar, or
more to taste

**Spice Paste**
10–15 dried red chillies,
sliced, soaked in hot
water to soften
8 shallots, chopped
3 cm (1 1/4 in) fresh
ginger, chopped
2 cloves garlic, chopped

1 Pat chicken pieces dry with a paper towel and put into a bowl. Sprinkle evenly with salt and turmeric, toss to mix well and set aside for 5 minutes.

2 Heat oil in a wok until very hot. Deep-fry the chicken pieces, a few at a time, until golden brown and crisp, 4–5 minutes. Drain the chicken on paper towels. Reserve 2 tablespoons of oil from the wok and pour out the rest of the oil.

3 To make the Spice Paste, grind chillies, shallots, ginger and garlic to a smooth paste in a spice grinder, blender or mortar and pestle.

4 Reheat the oil and stir-fry the Spice Paste, star anise, cloves and cinnamon over low–medium heat for about 4 minutes. Add the coconut milk, coconut cream, tomato paste and sugar and bring to the boil, stirring. Add the chicken pieces and simmer 5 minutes. Taste and add more sugar and salt if desired. Serve hot with plain rice or yellow rice.

Serves 4–6
Preparation time: **40 mins**
Cooking time: **20 mins**

# Indian Lamb Curry

3 tablespoons meat curry powder
$1/2$ teaspoon fennel powder
3 tablespoons water
3 tablespoons oil
4 cloves
4 cardamom pods, slit and bruised
1 cinnamon stick (about 5 cm/2 in)
1 whole star anise
1 large onion, sliced
3 cloves garlic, finely chopped
4 cm ($1^1/2$ in) fresh ginger, finely chopped
15 curry leaves
750 g ($1^3/4$ lbs) boneless lean lamb (or mutton), cut in bite-sized pieces
1 teaspoon salt
500 ml (2 cups) water, adding more as required
250 ml (1 cup) thick coconut milk (see note)
1 large onion, quartered
3 medium potatoes, quartered
1 teaspoon lime juice

1 Put the curry and fennel powders in a bowl and stir in water to make a paste. Set aside.

2 Heat the oil in a wok and add the cloves, cardamom, cinnamon and star anise. Stir-fry over low–medium heat for 1 minute. Add the sliced onion, garlic, ginger and curry leaves and stir-fry until the onion softens, 3–4 minutes. Add the curry paste and stir-fry for 1 minute.

3 Add the lamb or mutton and stir-fry until fragrant, about 5 minutes. Sprinkle with salt, add water and bring to the boil, then lower heat and simmer, stirring from time to time, until the meat is tender. If using mutton, the cooking time will be longer and it will be necessary to add a little water.

4 When the meat is tender, add the coconut milk, quartered onion and potatoes and continue cooking, stirring several times, until the potato is soft. Add a little water if the gravy starts to dry out before the potatoes are cooked. Add lime juice to taste and serve hot with plain white rice or pilau.

*For a healthier alternative, substitute 125 ml ($1/2$ cup) yoghurt and 125 ml ($1/2$ cup) low fat milk instead of coconut milk. Do not add lime juice if using yoghurt, as the yoghurt already adds a sour taste to the curry.*

Serves 6
Preparation time: **20 mins**
Cooking time: **1 hour**

# Pork Ribs Braised with Fermented Red Bean Curd

1 kg (2 lbs) meaty pork ribs, cut in bite-sized chunks
2 tablespoons oil
2 teaspoons finely chopped garlic
1 tablespoon finely chopped fresh ginger
3 tablespoons mashed fermented red bean curd (see page 5)
2 teaspoons sugar
2 tablespoons dark soy sauce
1 tablespoon rice wine
500–750 ml (2–3 cups) chicken stock (page 7)
$^1/_2$ teaspoon salt (optional)
1 teaspoon ground white pepper

**Marinade**
2 tablespoons rice wine
2 tablespoons sesame oil
1 tablespoon soy sauce
1 tablespoon cornflour

**1** Put pork ribs into a large bowl and sprinkle over the Marinade ingredients. Mix well. Set aside 10 minutes.
**2** Heat oil in a wok until very hot, then add pork ribs and stir-fry over very high heat until the ribs turn light brown, 2–3 minutes. Lower the heat to moderately hot, add garlic, ginger and stir-fry for a few seconds. Add the red bean curd and stir-fry 1 minute, then sprinkle over sugar and stir-fry for a few seconds. Add dark soy sauce and wine and stir. Next, put in 500 ml (2 cups) chicken stock and bring to the boil.
**3** Lower heat, cover the wok and simmer until the pork ribs are tender, 50–60 minutes, stirring several times so the ribs cook evenly. Add more stock if the sauce threatens to dry up before the pork is tender. Taste and add salt if desired, then sprinkle with white pepper and transfer to a serving dish.

Serves 4–6
Preparation time: **10 mins + 10 mins marinating**
Cooking time: **50 mins**

# Stir-fried Beef with Ginger and Egg

300 g (10 oz) beef fillet
  or striploin
1 tablespoon cornflour
60 ml ($^1/_4$ cup) oil
4 cm (1$^1/_2$ in) young ginger, cut in matchstick
  shreds
4 stalks spring onions,
  coarsely chopped
60 ml ($^1/_4$ cup) water
1 egg, lightly beaten

**Marinade**

1 tablespoon rice wine
1 tablespoon soy sauce
1 tablespoon oyster
  sauce
1 teaspoon sugar
$^1/_2$ teaspoon ground
  white pepper

1 Chill the beef in the freezer for 15 minutes, then cut across the grain into very thin slices.

2 Put the beef into a bowl, sprinkle with cornflour and toss to coat well. Add all the Marinade ingredients and mix well. Marinate for 30 minutes.

3 Heat the oil in a wok for 30 seconds. When moderately hot, add the ginger slices and stir-fry until golden and crisp, about 1 minute. Remove and drain on paper towel.

4 Increase the heat and stir-fry beef over very high heat, 1 minute. Add spring onions and stir-fry 15 seconds. Add water, then immediately pour in the egg and stir until set, about 5 seconds. Transfer immediately to a serving dish, garnish with fried ginger and serve with hot steamed white rice.

Serves 4
Preparation time: **20 mins + 30 mins marinating**
Cooking time: **5 mins**

# Gula Melaka
## (Sago Pearls with Coconut Cream and Palm Sugar)

180 g (1 cup) dried sago
  pearls (see note)
2 litres (8 cups) water
1 tablespoon milk
250 ml (1 cup) coconut
  cream
Pinch of salt

**Palm Sugar Syrup**
125 g ($^1/_2$ cup) palm
  sugar, finely chopped
185 ml ($^3/_4$ cup) water
2 pandan leaves, raked
  with a fork, tied in a knot

Serves 6
Preparation time: **10 mins**
Cooking time: **20 mins**

1 Put the sago in a sieve and shake over the sink to dislodge any loose starch. Bring the water to the boil in a large saucepan. Slowly pour in sago, stirring constantly with a wooden spoon. Boil uncovered, stirring occasionally, until sago pearls turn transparent, 10–12 minutes.
2 Tip the sago into a large wire mesh sieve and hold under cold running water to wash away the starch, about 45 seconds. Shake sieve until liquid has gone, then stir through the milk. Transfer to 6 glass serving dishes. When cool, refrigerate.
3 Make the Palm Sugar Syrup by combining the palm sugar, water and pandan leaf in a small saucepan. Bring to the boil, stirring until sugar dissolves. Simmer until syrup has reduced to 125 ml ($^1/_2$ cup). Remove pandan leaves and set aside to cool.
4 Transfer the palm sugar syrup and coconut cream to 2 small jugs. Add salt to the coconut cream. Serve with chilled sago, adding syrup and coconut cream to taste.

*Sago pearls* are tiny dried balls of sago obtained by grinding the pith of the sago palm to a paste and pressing it through a sieve. It is glutinous, with little taste, and is often used in Asian desserts. Sago pearls should not be confused with sago paste, which is starchy and sticky.

# Bubor Gandum
## (Wheat Grain Dessert with Coconut Milk and Palm Sugar)

100 g ($^1/_2$ cup) *gandum* (whole wheat grains), covered with boiling water, soaked 2 hours, drained
1$^1/_2$ litres (6 cups) water
500 ml (2 cups) thick coconut milk
$^1/_4$ teaspoon salt
50 g ($^1/_4$ cup) palm sugar, finely chopped
2 pandan leaves, raked with a fork, knotted
2 tablespoons white sugar, or more to taste

**1** Put the *gandum* and water in a large saucepan and bring to the boil, stirring several times. Cover and simmer, stirring occasionally for 1 hour.
**2** Add the coconut milk, salt, palm sugar and pandan leaves. Bring to the boil, lower heat and simmer uncovered. Stir occasionally until grains are soft and the liquid has greatly reduced, about 1$^1/_2$ hours.
**3** Taste and add sugar as desired. Discard the pandan leaves, transfer to four bowls and serve warm or at room temperature.

*Gandum are dried whole wheat grains that are boiled in water for use in Asian desserts; they are sold in Asian supermarkets.*

Serves 4
Preparation time: **2 hours**
Cooking time: **2$^1/_2$ hours**

# Chendol

230 g (1 cup) ready made
  chendol jelly strips
750 ml (3 cups) thick
  coconut milk

**Palm Sugar Syrup**
125 g ($^1/_2$ cup) palm
  sugar, chopped
1 tablespoon sugar
185 ml ($^3/_4$ cup) water

Makes 4 servings
Preparation time: **10 mins**
Cooking time: **20 mins**

1 Rinse the chendol jelly, drain and refrigerate.
2 To prepare the Palm Sugar Syrup, place both lots of sugar and water in a saucepan then simmer until the sugar has dissolved and the mixture thickens slightly. Set aside to cool then refrigerate.
3 To serve, rinse the chendol jelly in fresh water, drain and divide equally between 4 glasses or serving bowls. In each glass or serving bowl, add 1–2 tablespoons of the Palm Sugar Syrup, then top with 125 ml ($^1/_2$ cup) of thick coconut milk.

*Chendol jelly strips* are short, green and made from rice flour. Pandan extract or green food colouring is used to give the jelly strips their colour. Chendol jelly strips are sold in packets and are available in super-markets.

# List of Recipes